Around a World We Found A Most Amazing Town

Normous the elephant gathered together his six dear friends, Honey the bee, Goldie the butterfly, Gracie the swan, two sweet mice, Sugar and Spice and Greenie the frog.

They would hold a contest to find the best and most enjoyable town for children. A map would also be created so all children could easily find their way to the town.

As Normous and his friends traveled from North to South and East to West, ten towns were entered in their contest. One had balloons for riding up high, another had kites all dotting the sky. The town they chose had children whose hearts were aglow, for success in this town they truly did know.

As you read on you will know their secret to success.

To learn more about the children, the school, and the town that inspired this tale visit the web pages at the back of this book. You will catch a glimpse of what over 500,000 children have learned to help their creativity and intelligence flow with ease.

To His Holiness Maharishi Mahesh Yogi

Ridgley, Yamuna
   Around and Around We Found
   A Most Amazing Town / Yamuna Ridgley
   Summary: Normous the elephant gathered his 6 friends.
   They decided to search for a town that all children
   would flourish in and love. A contest was held and
   the town that won had children who succeeded in many
   endeavors because their creativity flowed with ease.

   ISBN-978-1502779991

1) Characters-Fiction.
2) Sunny Town-Fiction.
3) Stories in Rhyme

©2015 Yamuna Ridgley.
All Rights Reserved, ISBN
Printed in the United States of America

Around and Around We Found A Most Amazing Town

by Yamuna Ridgley

Dear children, you're right on time,
for a tale I'll tell you in rhyme.
Seven friends we are,
who traveled very far,
in search of a city, to win our star.
A contest we will hold.
The details will unfold.

They call me Normous the puppet,
I am the one who can trumpet.
My friends right here are dear.
Goldie the butterfly, Honey the bee,
a pair I'm sure you'll like to see.

And two sweet mice,
who are very nice.
Here is Sugar, and there is Spice.

High in the sky,
Gracie will fly.
A bird of great fame
with a very kind name.

Meet and Greet Greenie the frog,
a champ who makes his home on a log.

Seven puppets we are,
searching very far,
to give a city our star.

Many a town we would find.
'Ten' were of a special kind.
One had lollipops handed to guests.

Another had clowns we put to a test.
All funny bones here
were among the best.

A third had breezes all blowing their trees.

A fourth had slides right into the seas.

The fifth hung tinsel and lights for a show.

A tenth had chalk, that covered their walks.
A contest for all on the neighborhood blocks.

North, South, East and West
my friends and I
sought out the best.

Gliding, soaring, taking the lead,
Gracie saw towns from the skies
we would need.

Will one stand apart
and win every heart?

PUPPETS VOTING

The drum was rolling, the buglers were blowing.
Our votes we cast for a winner at last!

Now turn the page,
its name will be
on a map created
for you to see.

All can visit this town at last
which seems to be winning
all hearts very fast.

What makes us sing its fame?
Why Sunny is its name.

With photos on their mind,
an image they would find.
From wiggling toes,
to "hold that pose,"
they seem to place in many shows.

They're tennis champs indeed!
Who can match their speed?

Each move is a treat,
so hard to beat.
Are wings on their feet?

In choral reading, voices are meeting,
the judges insist they're great at competing.

With the town in our heart,
the awards we must start.

They've glittered and glowed, tickled our toes,
and helped us laugh right up to our nose.

We were so pleased to see
what every child can be.
When filled with courage and love,
success will soar above.

For us indeed it was fun!
Sunny Town you shine like the sun!

Yamuna Ridgley lives with her family in Iowa. She is an artist and a writer and has been a teacher and a director of a Montessori school.

During the Summer she enjoys hiking around the lakes and biking on the beautiful trails through the parks. Additional favorite activities are painting the flowers in her gardens and creating felt collages of playful scenes.

She would like you to know that the story in this book was inspired by an actual town, the school children and a mental technique that they use to unfold their inner creativity, intelligence and happiness.

If you would like to learn more about this town, the children and their remarkable achievements the following web pages are listed below.

---

discoverfairfield.org/fairfield
travelfairfield.com

Made in the USA
Middletown, DE
26 July 2015